A Gentle Wind

Karen Field

A publication of

Eber & Wein Publishing
Pennsylvania

A Gentle Wind

Copyright © 2020 by Karen Field

All rights reserved under the International and Pan-American copyright conventions. No part of this book may be reproduced, stored in a retrieval system, or transmitted in any form, electronic, mechanical, or by other means, without written permission of the author.

Library of Congress
Cataloging in Publication Data

ISBN 978-1-60880-657-7

Proudly manufactured in the United States of America by

Eber & Wein Publishing
Pennsylvania

*This book is lovingly dedicated
to the memory
of my mother and father*

About the Author

Karen Field grew up in a village along the majestic Hudson River in New York where she, her grandparents, parents, and siblings shared the house her grandfather built. In the summer she spent her time sailing with her family on her father's boat, The Albatross. She attended the Hastings schools and graduated from the Berkeley School and Elizabeth Seton College. Her interest in writing surfaced at an early age, and her father would often take great delight in reciting her poetry. <u>A Gentle Wind</u> represents her earlier work as well as her most recent and intense poetry now available on most major websites. Living her entire life in New York, today she resides in a small town and continues to write some of her most extraordinary poems. This collection of poetry reflects the author's unique writing style as she expresses her love for the beauty and tranquility in nature.

Contents

Petals...1
Summer..2
A Red Rose..4
July...6
Winter Rose..8
Peacock Blue..6
In Clover...8
Essence..9
Springtime..10
So Long Ago...13
Breath of Spring..14
Satin Flowers..15
Weeping Willow..16
Summertime..17
Blue-Silver Sea...18
A Scarlet Rose..19
Summery Things...20
Summer Cottage...23
The Robin Won't Sing...............................24
I Gather Wildflowers.................................25
Rose Moon...26
Deep Velvet Green.....................................27
Soft Winds..28
Field of Flowers..29
Blackbird...30
A Lover's Lament.......................................31
A Field of Lavender...................................32
Spring...34
A Song on the Winds of Time................35

Blue Shawl... 36
Paper-Mâché... 37
Monet's Garden... 39
Tapestry and Lace.. 40
Summer Winds.. 41
A Love Letter... 42
Path of Gold.. 44
Lilacs on the Hill... 45
Summer's Last Rose... 46
Love.. 47
Blue Breeze... 48

A Gentle Wind

A Gentle Wind

Petals

The beauty of a flower
Is quite divine.
The petals are so lovely
I shall make them mine.

One petal has a dewdrop;
Another blew away.
I shall keep the others
In my heart all day.

Spring is such a pretty time
With water lilies by Monet.
Lovers watch them floating by
And falling petals fly away.

Karen Field

Summer

The day is there,
Quiet and still,
My refuge
With the wind on the hill.

I hail the summer
For its blossoms and song;
It caresses the willows
Where young lovers long.

I cast a wild rose
Upon summer's breeze
And gather the petals
By the windless trees.

A Gentle Wind

A Red Rose

Autumn winds blow lightly in the meadow;
Sparrows soar in the asphaltic sky.
Leaves crumble upon the earth,
And lovers with the winds faintly sigh.

Fading sunshine and wildflowers
Wrap around the river's edge.
In the midst of gentle breezes,
Songbirds perch on a window ledge.

The day lingers in the shadows of night;
Darkness creeps upon the ground.
Beneath a full moon veiled by haze,
A red rose drifts until it's found.

Karen Field

July

There's a dazzling lily in pink.
The sky is cerulean blue.
The meadow is mint green;
Windflowers waltz softly to you.

Lovers chase a white butterfly.
Dandelion puffs blow over me.
Violets gather by a summer cottage.
A lady with a rose looks out to sea.

Playful breezes dance around.
The surf is gentle this time.
Sunbathers love July.
Summer is divine.

A Gentle Wind

Winter Rose

The breath of winter is gray.
Blackbirds perched are few.
Spring peeks through the snow
In pretty shades of blue.

Dark days of winter fade.
The tulips blossom outright.
Icicles turn to drops of dew.
Frost flowers are a sight.

Warm winds catch a butterfly.
The sparrows cheerfully sing.
I see a winter rose
So lovely there in spring.

Karen Field

Peacock Blue

The day was peacock blue.
The ladybug was on the screen.
Summer wore her old straw hat.
The meadow turned lime green.

The sunflower was solid gold.
The water lily was by Monet.
July caught a butterfly's wing.
The windflower just blew away.

Karen Field

In Clover

Love is a meadow
With a stream flowing through;
Spring is its domain
As the rose to the dew!

It buds spontaneously
In clover here!
The gardenias are potted,
And the doves are near.

A bouquet shall be ready
Sometime in June
When all the flowers
Shall be in full bloom!

And for you, love,
They shall be as you are,
Soft petals falling
Beneath a star!

A Gentle Wind

Essence

Behold the night
When the moon is gold
That life and living
Shall unfold.

The will of the heart
And its utmost desire
Shall not be left
In mulch and mire.

The rose is the essence
Of passion and love
It lives in the soul
Forever thereof.

Karen Field

Springtime

*Love is a soft
And quiet thing—
A gift that blossoms
Often bring.*

*You will know it
By each pretty bloom
That flourishes
By the month of June.*

*There will be a flower
Especially for you,
Perhaps a rose
With drops of dew.*

*And by the end
Of a springtime day,
There will be another
Along your way!*

A Gentle Wind

So Long Ago

A glimmering diamond
A kiss
A cut of passion
Bestowed upon my soul
Your lips pressed gently
Upon my cheek
Warm and tender
So long ago
A loving embrace
Forever lingers deep in me
The sun dips, slips slowly away
Dripping across a shade of gold
A lovely season in the midst
Glistening in the sunlit haze
With a slight and sultry
Summer wind
My heart is melting
Breathing in the scent of you
In the afterglow within

Karen Field

Breath of Spring

When I walk through spring
The tulips always greet me there.
It's the grandest garden tour;
The cherry blossoms swear.

The daffodils are in abundance.
Wildflowers seem to pass me by.
Spring is a bursting bubble.
Miss Lily adores the butterfly.

Lovers run through a lavender field;
They gather a pretty purple bouquet.
Windflowers blow ever so softly.
I feel the breath of spring today.

Satin Flowers

There's a red rose in the sand.
Starfish and driftwood wash ashore.
Lovers breathe the seaward wind.
The surf ebbs forevermore.

Silver grass softly sways.
The pond in the meadow is still.
A slight breeze blows aloft.
It's summer on the sunlit hill.

Some autumn leaves won't let go.
Satin flowers make a lovely bouquet.
Blackbirds perch upon a leafless tree;
The weeping willows behold the day.

Karen Field

Weeping Willow

*I will embrace your essence
And hold you lightly in my breeze
On long hot summer days
Beneath my swaying leaves.*

*I will be your canopy
In the haze and misty rain
And shelter you from a stormy sky
Before the sun shines once again.*

*I will wrap my flowing limbs
Around you tenderly
And caress your weeping soul
That blows through me.*

A Gentle Wind

Summertime

*There is a cellist in the meadow
Playing a timeless melody.
A butterfly flutters by a windless willow;
Summer waits there patiently.*

*Spring bestows its precious blossoms
And the prettiest ones are so divine.
A bouquet waits for lovers there
To behold in summertime.*

Karen Field

Blue-Silver Sea

My hat is a parasol.
The sun is ablaze.
Summer is sublime
On long golden days.

Pearl white ripples
Splash over me.
The sea bird soars
Above the blue-silver sea.

The heart of the fisherman
Is sometimes forlorn;
He casts his nets
At the sliver of dawn.

There are pretty wildflowers
Beyond the dune
That the night beholds
For the strawberry moon.

A Gentle Wind

A Scarlet Rose

Oh my darling, my love divine,
So many days and nights linger to eternity.
I hail the moment of your swift return,
While my heart weeps unbeknownst to thee.
Many moons pass in the twilight of my years;
The days grow long and tiresome with time.
Each breath of a sweet scent I breathe for thee,
Though today is yielding beauty's sign.
The eves ebb slowly beneath dimmed sunsets,
As long nights creep in my darkest hour of wintertime:
Oh tomorrow may reveal the solemn truth, I trust,
So long as these sullen days and nights are mine.
Then who shall be my dearest love? I ask of you.
A scarlet rose for thee shall be my lover's rue.

Karen Field

Summery Things

There are butterflies and silver grass
In fields of green-sea blue,
And with all the flowers to behold
I cherish the ones from you.

I roam and gather summery things
Like the sand pebbles you gave to me,
And when summer turns to gold
I shall return them to the sea.

A Gentle Wind

Summer Cottage

Summer is a pink bouquet.
The sky is lavender blue.
The meadow is a sea of green.
Windflowers blow forever to you.

There's a caterpillar on a maple leaf.
A lady in lace sits on a dune by the sea.
Weeping willows catch a gentle breeze.
You gather pretty red roses for me.

Lovers chase a purple butterfly.
The parasols are sage and gold.
Violets cling to the white picket fence.
It's a summer cottage to behold.

Karen Field

The Robin Won't Sing

I'm in a quandary
In the middle of spring.
The brook isn't babbling;
The robin won't sing.

The wild roadside flowers
Instinctively don't care;
They unearth pretty gardens
And spread out everywhere.

The day is cobalt blue.
The sunflower droops outright.
A spring breeze goes still.
The butterfly's a sight.

I listen for a meadowlark
To sing its song to me.
Spring is just so symptomatic
The lilies rush out to sea.

Springtime is a charming place,
A respite from the storm.
It is sometimes contradictory
When evening comes at dawn.

A Gentle Wind

I Gather Wildflowers

*I stand still
Beside the day
Between the rain
With little to say.*

*I go to the stream
And stand with the day;
With summer by my side
I want to stay.*

*I rejoice with the birds;
They chirp away.
Lovers dance;
The willows sway.*

*I run through the meadow
After the day;
I gather wildflowers
For you today.*

Karen Field

Rose Moon

*It was the rose moon of summer
That crept along my shadow there,
And the winds like waves of silk
Blew softly through the midnight air.*

*Oh the time seemed less forgiving
Of what I knew of love before;
Though when you perched upon my soul,
I heard a songbird there once more.*

*Love was the sweetest bud in bloom—
A myriad of sunlit gold.
And with a breath of English Miss
The garden seemed to just unfold.*

*Oh those warm and southerly winds
Embraced us gently by the sea,
And beneath a moonlit summer eve
There my true love encountered me.*

A Gentle Wind

Deep Velvet Green

*I remember you so very long ago—
A distant memory lingering
In the shadows of my soul.
It seems to fade in the morning light;
It is all there is for now, for me
In the midst of a beautiful summer
With the sun burning like fire
Across the rippling of the sea.
It is a longing for a song
Haunting deep within my soul
To sing to only you, my love,
Upon dunes of glistening gold.
I shall feel your spirit forever
Blowing in the whispering winds—
In days of deep velvet green
Along weathered paths of time
In the blossoming gardens in spring.
There your essence shall forever be
Quietly breathing with nature
Ever so tenderly.*

Karen Field

Soft Winds

Soft winds blow the petals aloft
As you clutch the roses to your heart.
A bouquet so eloquent
In the garden shall not depart.

A season's mystifying scent—
Soft fragrant mists,
Light showers,
Blossoms and amethyst.

Wisps of lavender
Brush upon your soul,
And the weeping willows
Gently blow.

A Gentle Wind

Field of Flowers

Oh do not weep, young heart,
In the magical garden to be
And do not shed sorrow's tear
Upon the old maplewood tree.

Lilacs and violets are many
In a meadow of peaceful resign.
Lovers go to gather them
To behold forever in time.

A butterfly dances on a daffodil;
A slight breeze catches spring.
Satin flowers are ever so lovely.
The songbirds come to sing.

Pink petals fall upon the earth
From the cherry blossom trees,
And stirring in the scarlet sky
Twirls a stream of velvet leaves.

The April springtime winds
Stay warm and gentle still
For a pretty field of flowers
And the ones left on the hill.

Karen Field

Blackbird

The blackbird on its perch
Beckons to the dawn
Expressly in its quest
That early April morn!

The blackbird on its perch
Broke the quiet sound
With its sleek demeanor—
May is in a lurch!

The blackbird on its perch
Instinctively won't wait.
There's chirping in the nest
And harvest filled with bait.

A Gentle Wind

A Lover's Lament

*The summer breathes in me
The enchantment of love—
A kiss, an embrace.
Oh how the season lingers
Passionately with the willows
Where lovers love to love
In nature's subtle breezes.*

*Oh what would a meadow be
Without the weeping willow trees
Or songbirds
As they graciously sing
For lovers eternally?*

*A lady in blue gathers a rose
From Monet's garden,
Clutches it to her bosom,
Then quietly weeps
As she passes by.*

*I feel the gentleness of early autumn
As it breathes with the willows
Upon summer's path,
Where a lover's lament
Is emphatically etched
By a rose adrift with falling leaves
Blowing softly in the wind.*

Karen Field

A Field of Lavender

Petals from a purple orchid
Drift softly on a sunlit morn.
In the garden some blossoms are full;
The others are wilted and worn.

I kneel closely by the wistful ones
There with a butterfly flitting away.
I dream of a field of lavender
And all that I'll gather today.

Oh the willows are listless and weepy
In a far-off, distant shore,
And there in the warm and seaward winds,
I embrace them all once more.

Karen Field

Spring

The garden is a century old.
The flowers are brand new.
I shall pick them in late spring
Then give them all to you.

I know the thing I feel
Is in the garden there.
It blossoms in each flower
When spring is in the air.

The evening falls so quietly
And April doesn't care.
The golden moon lay on the hill
For lovers everywhere.

A Gentle Wind

A Song on the Winds of Time

*There you are among the roses
In a garden so divine,
A place where magical beauty reigns,
A song on the winds of time.*

*A splash of color,
A light misty spray,
A floral fantasy
Bestowed upon the day.*

*A flame burns from a candle,
A memoir left for thee.
Soft winds in a meadow
Blow ever so tenderly.*

Karen Field

Blue Shawl

Warm breezes spill in from afar
And caress young jonquils on the hill.
Oh spring is such a dreamful time
When the day is lovely, quiet and still.

Songbirds sing in a tall white birch,
And water lilies drift by a willow tree.
Pretty violets grace a faraway meadow
Where a gentle wind embraces me.

I feel the light, misty rain of June.
A gold butterfly flutters as it passes by.
There in the purple lavender field
The mellow winds of springtime sigh.

Alone on a veranda by the moonlit sea,
Young lovers cast their first rose on the shore.
A blue shawl wraps it in a soft sea breeze,
And there in the wind lives love evermore.

A Gentle Wind

Paper-Mâché

*I celebrate a delightful springtime day
In a white sundress clutching roses your way;
The pink magnolias gracefully sway
By a pond in a lovely meadow in May.*

*Summer blew in through the willows today
With soft breezes on the pier by the bay.
Oh, the flowers are so pretty, I say,
And the lily pads look like those by Monet.*

*The days are enchanting as a picture essay,
As warm nightly winds blow gently astray.
Lovers embrace in a midsummer play,
And the players are the lovers they portray.*

*The flowers will slowly shrivel and decay,
But warm summer breezes keep stealing away.
Autumn creeps in without much delay,
And the roses I clutch are made of paper-mâché.*

A Gentle Wind

Monet's Garden

At the edge of Monet's water lily pond
Breathes a glorious morning in Giverny today.
The essence of his magnificent garden
Overflows with the prettiest flowers by May.

The roses are in blossom in the sunlit glow
And tales of romance are made of gold;
The songbirds sing their loveliest song
And the beauty of springtime days unfold.

The romanticist searches his heart's desire
And recites his most treasured prose
To the lady in blue in Monet's garden
Holding a beautiful long-stemmed rose.

Karen Field

Tapestry and Lace

April is a winter sweater
Worn upon its coolest day;
It becomes a fine silk shawl
By the lovely month of May.

The flowers there are many
Upon each patch of space.
The colors are diverse and pretty
In springtime's tapestry and lace.

Do behold its beauty now;
It comes and goes so fast.
Pick a special spring bouquet;
Nothing ever seems to last.

A Gentle Wind

Summer Winds

The moon shall light the earth;
The stars shall sparkle upon the sea.
Winds rush off the cliffs;
Soft breezes return to thee.

In quiet calmness by the shore,
The sea ebbs gently at dawn
With summer at the water's edge,
The sky without a storm.

The morning sun is melting away;
Sand brushes lightly upon your soul.
Deep within the summer winds,
It drips of glistening gold.

You long to bathe in the endless waves,
To breathe and taste the morning dew.
The season entices the stars and moon;
The night embraces you.

Karen Field

A Love Letter

To my dearest love divine
You shall forever be only mine.
I behold the rose from you within;
It lives forever in the wind.

Your words embrace me tenderly;
I feel them by the willow tree.
It's a timeless love affair, my dear;
The songbirds sing for us to hear.

Karen Field

Path of Gold

I walk along a path
Between the shadows of the trees;
Beneath their bending limbs
I seek their warm and gentle breeze.

I love the wonder of spring,
And in its beauty I behold
The scent of early morning dew—
The center of its soul.

I walk along a path of emerald
To a glistening path of gold;
I bathe in wet sand by the sea—
Its soft and gentle winds I hold.

A Gentle Wind

Lilacs on the Hill

*The tulips are in bud
In their peaceful place.
They wake up when it's time
In beauty and in grace.*

*Spring unchains the earth
And sprouts its own design.
It breaks out in the garden
And climbs the ivy vine.*

*It dwells along a picket fence
And on a countryside,
And in a field of misty rain
Where daffodils reside.*

*June is just a moon away
After May's big thrill,
But summer is the one
With lilacs on the hill.*

Karen Field

Summer's Last Rose

Oh how the gentle winds of August
Embrace the meadow by the sea.
The willows brush upon your soul
And there your heart weeps quietly.

A flame flickers on the edge of time,
And a memoir is washed upon the shore.
It's tied with an old fisherman's twine,
And it's buried in the sand evermore.

Love is a magical blue butterfly,
And it's etched in its destiny.
Young lovers catch it on a starlit eve
With summer's last rose by the sea.

A Gentle Wind

Love

Oh it's a sleepless and gentle wind of summer
That begins to slowly stir within my heart anew.
It weaves its way from the weeping willows
And through the meadow we once knew.
When the night is settled in its deepest, darkest hour,
I hear the winds in the garden breathe a wistful sigh.
And beneath the galaxy of a thousand stars alight,
I see the windflowers softly blow on couples passing by.
What then, my love, shall I humbly ask of you,
While the moon shines its brightest on lovers everywhere?
Oh the whispering winds of summer embrace the soul of me,
And I seem to love you even more when love seems so unfair.
So, until you are mine once again to lovingly forgive,
I shall wait for your return as long as love shall live.

Karen Field

Blue Breeze

Summer
Something
Rare
A
Jewel
So
Serene
Surreal
Like
Pearls
That
Entice
And
Enchant
My
Soul
With
A
Leaf
Aflutter
In
A
Velvet
Field
And
A
Blackbird
With
Blades
Of
Ribbons

A Gentle Wind

*Cascading
In
The
Softness
Of
Your
Breeze

Oh
Time
Endless
Endless
Time
Goes
On
And
You
And
I
Wallow
In
It
For
So
Long
While
Ripples
Of
White
Diamonds
And
Silver
Drops*

Karen Field

Ebb
With
The
Cool
White
Foam

Lovers
Touch
Then
Fade
In
The
Quietness
Of
Idle
Play
And
The
Blue
Breeze
Goes
On
And
On
In
Summer
And
Time
Endless
Time
Forever

www.ingramcontent.com/pod-product-compliance
Lightning Source LLC
Chambersburg PA
CBHW040311050426
42450CB00019B/3461